MEASURE UP MATH

DISTANCE

Chris Woodford

Gareth Stevens
Publishing

Please visit our website, www.garethstevens.com. For a free color catalog of all our high-quality books, call toll-free 1-800-542-2595 or fax 1-877-542-2596.

Library of Congress Cataloging-in-Publication Data

Woodford, Chris.
Distance / Chris Woodford.
    p. cm. — (Measure up math)
Includes index.
ISBN 978-1-4339-7438-0 (pbk.)
ISBN 978-1-4339-7439-7 (6-pack)
ISBN 978-1-4339-7437-3 (lib. bdg.)
1. Length measurement—Juvenile literature. 2. Distances—Measurement—Juvenile literature. I. Title.
QC102.W664 2013
530.8'1—dc23

2011052766

Published in 2013 by
Gareth Stevens Publishing
111 East 14th Street, Suite 349
New York, NY 10003

© 2013 Brown Bear Books Ltd

For Brown Bear Books Ltd:
Editorial Director: Lindsey Lowe
Managing Editor: Tim Harris
Children's Publisher: Anne O'Daly
Art Director: Jeni Child
Designer: Lynne Lennon
Picture Manager: Sophie Mortimer
Production Director: Alastair Gourlay

Picture Credits:
Key: t = top, b = bottom, c = center
Front Cover: Shutterstock: Bill Lawson
Interior: Corbis: Micro Discover 16; **Getty Images:** Alex Livese/ALLSPORT 22; **Shutterstock:** Alhovik 12r, Jeff Banke 11b, Gualtiero Foffi 18, Flooter 8, Kimberly Hall 12c, Dmitry Kalinovsky 14, Cosmin Manci 11t, Mondkey Business Images 7, Nekephotos 10; **Thinkstock:** Hemera 23; US Department of Defence: 25. All other artworks and photographs Brown Bear Books.
Brown Bear Books has made every attempt to contact the copyright holder. If anyone has any information could they please contact smortimer@windmillbooks.co.uk

All Artworks © Brown Bear Books Ltd

Manufactured in the United States of America
1 2 3 4 5 6 7 8 9 12 11 10

CPSIA compliance information: Batch #BRS12GS: For further information contact Gareth Stevens, New York, New York at 1-800-542-2595.

CONTENTS

What is distance? 4

Measuring distance with fingers
and feet 6

Imperial measurement 8

Metric measurement 10

Different ways to measure
distance 12

Measuring very small distances 14

Tiny, tiny distances 16

Longer distances 18

Distances on maps 20

Measuring miles 22

Distances at sea 24

Space distances 26

HANDS ON:

How long is your street? 28

Glossary 30

Find out more 31

Index 32

WHAT IS DISTANCE?

Have you ever gazed up at the Moon and wondered how far away it is? Or looked at a map of your town and thought about how someone drew it? Perhaps you might have wondered how long a whale is. Questions like that involve distance.

Length and height

Distance is a measurement of how long, tall, or far away something is. One kind of distance is length. Length is the distance from one end of an object

▼ The Empire State Building in New York City is 1,250 feet high.

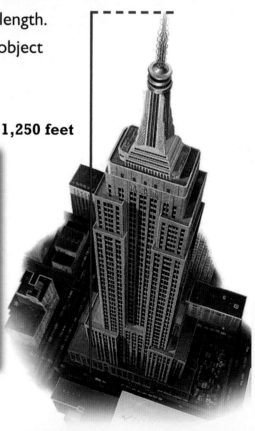

1,250 feet

DISTANCE AND LENGTH

Distance and length are the same thing.
This line is 1 inch long. ——————
1 foot = 12 inches
1 yard = 3 feet = 36 inches
1 mile = 1,760 yards = 5,280 feet
        = 63,360 inches

to the other. Height is another kind of distance. It is a measure of how tall something is. The height of a building is the distance from the ground to the very top.

Ways to measure

People can measure distance along a straight line using all kinds of tools. These tools include rulers made of wood, plastic, or metal; tapes, which bend easily; and laser beams (strong rays of light). Tapes can even be used to measure around corners. All these things help people measure distances on land, at sea, and even far out in space.

There are lots of reasons why we need to measure distance. You might want to know if a pair of jeans will be long enough to fit your legs or big enough around the waist. A family driving to another town needs to know how far away it is so they can figure out how much gas to put in the tank and when they will arrive.

▼ A blue whale measures 100 feet long. Compare it to the height of an adult human—about 6 feet.

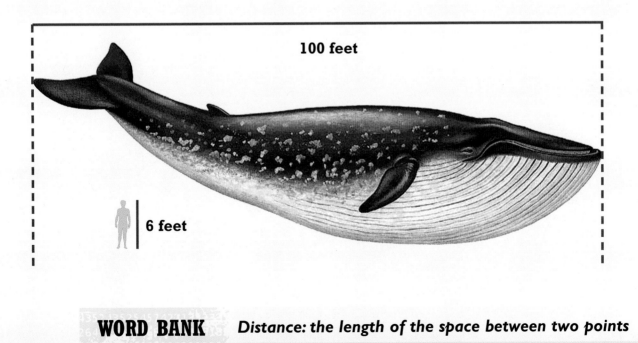

100 feet

6 feet

WORD BANK   *Distance: the length of the space between two points*

MEASURING DISTANCE WITH FINGERS AND FEET

In ancient times, people used parts of their body to measure distance. About 5,000 years ago, the ancient Egyptians invented a measurement called the cubit. A cubit was the distance from the tip of a person's middle finger to the elbow.

The Egyptians did not go around measuring things with their arms, though. They used sticks cut to the length of a cubit.

▼ The ancient Egyptians built massive structures like this pyramid. They needed to be able to measure distances accurately to make sure their buildings did not fall down.

HOW MANY CUBITS?

Imagine you and your family are ancient Egyptians. Get an adult to stretch out his or her arm from the middle finger to the elbow. That measurement is a cubit. Now try measuring some things around your home in cubits. You could try measuring your bed, your sofa, or the length of a table.

+ − = x + = x + − = x + − = x + − =

▼ Ancient measurements

A: 1 cubit (the forearm)

B: 16 finger widths = 1 foot

C: 1 uncia = about 1 inch

D: 1 foot = about 12 inches

Ancient Greeks and Romans

The ancient Greeks lived about 2,500 years ago. They measured distance with the width of their fingers. Sixteen fingers was roughly equal to the length of a person's foot. This is how the measurement the foot got its name.

The ancient Romans lived shortly after the Greeks. Instead of using fingers, like the Greeks, the Romans used the width of their thumb. They called this measurement an uncia. The modern word "inch" comes from that same word. The Romans found that an adult's foot was usually about 12 inches long. That is why there are still 12 inches in a foot.

WORD BANK *Cubit: an ancient measurement; the length of the forearm*

IMPERIAL MEASUREMENT

Through the ages, people have measured distances in different ways. In England about 1,000 years ago, people measured an inch by placing three ears of barley side by side. The distance across the three ears was one inch. The ancient Romans measured an inch using the width of their thumbs.

Confusing measurements

Different ways of measuring made it hard for people to buy and sell things. Suppose someone wanted to buy some cloth. If different traders used different measures,

▼ The four bases of a baseball field form a square. The sides of the square are 90 feet long.

90 feet

HOW LONG AND HOW FAR?

Here are some distances measured using the imperial system:

The height of a typical person = 5 feet 9 inches

How many inches is that?

The length of a family car = 18 feet

How many inches is that?

The length of a football field = 120 yards

How many feet is that?

Answers on page 31.

Los Angeles · New York

EARTH

25,000 miles

Key   The distance around Earth is 25,000 miles.

no one could tell how much cloth they were getting for their money. Measuring distance was equally confusing.

But several hundred years ago in Europe, during a time called the Middle Ages, people started to use the same measurements—the inch, foot, yard, and mile. This system of measuring is usually called the imperial system. People in many countries, including the United States, still use the imperial system.

1 inch

▲ People once measured an inch by placing three ears of barley side by side. It was not an accurate way to measure.

WORD BANK   *Foot: a distance equal to 12 inches*

METRIC MEASUREMENT

▶▶▶ **M**any people found the imperial system hard to remember. And every country had its own system for measuring distance. During the 18th century, some people in France came up with a simpler way to measure distances. Their system was based on a new measurement called the meter. France started to use this metric system in 1799.

Meters

The metric system (also called the International System, or SI system) is now used in most countries. One meter is 39 inches long, which is a little longer than a yard (3 feet, or 36 inches).

▶ **This signpost shows the distances to various cities in kilometers. It says that New York is 3,923 kilometers away.**

London 7,575km

PARIS 7,912KM

NEW YORK 3,923KM

FRANKFURT 8,057KM

Yellowknife 1,567

Ottawa 3,550km

042KM

St. John's nfld. 5,004km

Delhi 11,129

Los Angeles 1,740km

JOHANNESBURG 16,453KM

Other metric units

The metric system is easier to remember than the imperial system—there are 10 millimeters (mm) in a centimeter (cm), 100 centimeters in a meter (m), and 1,000 meters in a kilometer (km). One centimeter is a little less than half an inch, and one kilometer is just over half a mile.

FACT

The original meter—a bar made of platinum metal—is still kept in Paris, France.

▶ **TRY THIS**

+ − = x + − = x + − = x + − = x + − = −

THINK METRIC

This red line is 1 centimeter long. ▬

◀ **An adult flea is 3 millimeters long.**

▼ **An elephant is 3 meters high.**

1 centimeter = 10 millimeters
100 centimeters = 1 meter
1,000 meters = 1 kilometer

How tall are you (give your answer in meters and centimeters)?

How long is your little finger (centimeters and millimeters)?

How tall is a page of this book (centimeters and millimeters)?

+ − = x + − = x + − = x + − = − − = x +

WORD BANK *Meter: a metric measurement equal to about 3.3 feet*

DIFFERENT WAYS TO MEASURE DISTANCE

▶ Long, flexible tape measures and rigid 12-inch rulers are tools that can be used to measure distance.

▶▶▶ Everyone needs to measure things in exactly the same way. They do this by using a standard measuring tool, such as a ruler or a tape measure. A ruler is a piece of wood, plastic, or metal marked with exact measurements. A tape is marked in the same way, but it is bendy.

Rulers are usually about 1 foot (30 centimeters) or 1 yard (90 centimeters) long. One-yard rulers are called yardsticks. Another ruler—a meterstick—is 1 meter (39 inches) long.

CONVERTING FROM IMPERIAL TO METRIC

People often have to change imperial measurements into metric measurements, or metric into imperial measurements.

IMPERIAL TO METRIC

**1 inch = 2.5 centimeters,
    or 25 millimeters**

1 foot = 30 centimeters

1 yard = 90 centimeters

**1 mile = 1,600 meters,
    or 1.6 kilometers**

METRIC TO IMPERIAL

1 centimeter = 0.4 inch

**1 meter = 3 feet 3 inches,
    or 39 inches**

1 kilometer = 0.6 mile

**How many kilometers are there
    in 4 miles?**

**How many centimeters are there
    in 4 inches?**

**How many miles are there
    in 16 kilometers?**

Answers on page 31.

+ − = x + − = x + − = x + − = x + − = x + − = x + − = x + =

Longer distances

Rulers can be used to measure distances that are longer or shorter than the ruler itself. Most rulers are marked with smaller units—inches, centimeters, or millimeters. A person can measure longer things by moving the ruler along and counting how many times it fits into a distance.

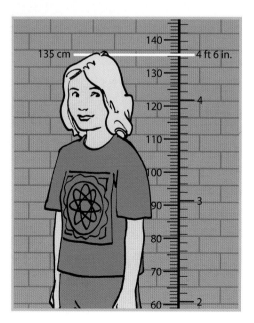

135 cm

140 — 4 ft 6 in.
130
120 — 4
110
100
90 — 3
80
70
60 — 2

▶ **This girl is 4 foot 6 inches,
or 135 centimeters, tall.**

WORD BANK   *Centimeter: one meter divided by 100*

15

MEASURING VERY SMALL DISTANCES

▲ An engineer is using a caliper to measure the width of a piece of machinery. This caliper has a digital display that indicates the width.

Sometimes people need to measure small distances on a map or the thickness of small objects. The best way to do this is with dividers, calipers, or gauges.

Dividers are like the compasses people use to draw circles. To measure the distance between two points on a map, the two legs of the dividers are opened and one leg is put on each point. Then the distance between the divider legs is measured against the map scale.

Calipers and gauges

The width of an apple or other small object may be measured by placing it in a caliper. When the apple is removed, a ruler may be used to measure the distance between the caliper legs.

A gauge has slots of different sizes cut into it. The width of a wire can be measured by matching it with the slot of the same size. Then the measurement can be read on the gauge.

▶ MICROMETER

A micrometer is a type of caliper with a built-in measuring scale. A micrometer is shaped like the letter C. It very accurately measures the width of an object placed between its jaws.

▼ **This diagram shows how a micrometer could be used to measure the width of a steel marble.**

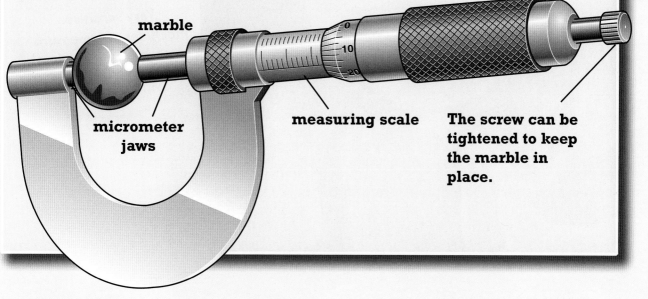

marble

micrometer jaws

measuring scale

The screw can be tightened to keep the marble in place.

WORD BANK *Gauge: a device for measuring small widths*

TINY, TINY DISTANCES

This is a picture of a weevil's head magnified 50 times. A weevil is a kind of insect.

It is possible for people to measure distances that are too small to see. The length of something like a tiny bug can be measured with a simple microscope, for example. A microscope is a special tool with lenses that make tiny objects appear much larger. Lenses are slices of polished and curved glass. Some microscopes have a ruler built into the eyepiece.

FACT
Very sensitive machines can measure distances smaller than a speck of dust.

Nanotechnology is one of the most exciting areas of science. It involves building new materials, medicines, and other things from incredibly tiny parts. Each part is just a few nanometers across. A nanometer (nm) is one-billionth of a meter. It is hard to imagine a distance so small, but a tiny speck of dust may be only about 3 nanometers wide. Put another way, if a nanometer were as big as the width of a pin head, a meter would be as far as the distance between Atlanta, Georgia, and Washington, DC!

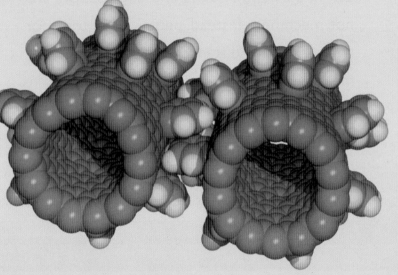

▲ Two tiny nanotubes made from minute particles called atoms.

The size of an object can be seen by lining it up with this ruler. Both the ruler and the object are magnified (made to look larger) by the microscope. Some microscope lenses magnify about 10 times normal size, while others magnify things about 1,500 times. Other microscopes have a micrometer built into them. By looking at the micrometer scale, it is possible to work out the object's size.

WORD BANK *Nanometer: a tiny distance, one billionth of a meter*

LONGER DISTANCES

Suppose a person wanted to plan the route of a freeway. Rulers and microscopes are not much help. Instead, people need tools for measuring long distances. In the past, people measured distances using clumsy metal chains. These chains were like huge folding rulers.

▼ **Miles and miles of road stretch out across a desert. Such long distances cannot be measured simply by using rulers or tapes.**

Measuring with chains

Each chain had 100 metal links. Each link was 8 inches (20 centimeters) long, so the whole chain stretched to about 66 feet (20 meters). People measured long distances by laying chains end to end. It took 80 chains to make 1 mile (1.6 kilometers).

FACT

Light from a theodolite's laser travels at 186,000 miles per second (300,000 km/s).

LASER RULERS

Earth does not have a flat, smooth surface. Hills, rivers, mountains, and valleys make it hard to measure distances with long chains. So people now measure long distances using theodolites. A theodolite can measure angles and distances very accurately. A theodolite sits on top of a tripod (a stand with three legs) to keep it steady. Another tripod, with a mirror on top, is placed at the point to be measured. A person presses a button. The theodolite fires a laser beam to the mirror, which bounces the beam back. A computer in the theodolite figures out how far away the mirror is and shows the result on a screen.

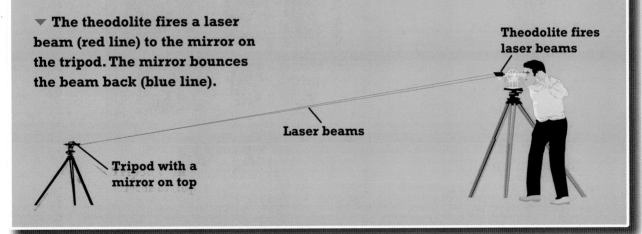

▼ The theodolite fires a laser beam (red line) to the mirror on the tripod. The mirror bounces the beam back (blue line).

Theodolite fires laser beams

Laser beams

Tripod with a mirror on top

WORD BANK   *Laser beam: a very strong, straight beam of light*

DISTANCES ON MAPS

Tools such as chains and theodolites are useful for planning highways and buildings. They are also very important for drawing maps. A map is a picture of a place seen from above. For a map to be useful, it must show where things are and how far away one thing is from another. Measuring distances is very important for making maps.

▶ A view of part of a town from above shows where all the buildings, roads, and railroads are.

▶ TRY THIS

+ − = x + − = x + − = x + − = x

WHERE ARE YOU?

This is a map of the town that is illustrated on the facing page.

Can you work out where Main Street is on the map?

Can you see where City Hall is on the map?

And can you work out where the town's mall is?

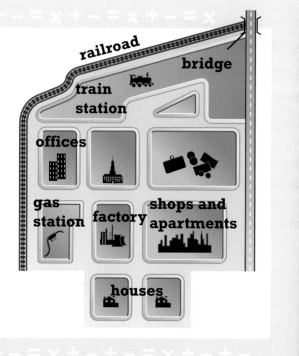

railroad

bridge

train station

offices

gas station factory shops and apartments

houses

+ − = x + − = x + − = x + − = x + − + − = x + − + −

Scales on maps

Maps usually have a scale (like a picture of a ruler) drawn on them. The scale shows how big the things on the map really are. A common scale is for 1 inch (2.5 cm) to equal 10 miles (16 km). So a street that is 1 inch long on the map is 10 miles long in real life.

bridge

train station

railroad

shops and apartments

mall

offices

City Hall

MAIN STREET

factory

gas station

houses

houses

MEASURING MILES

▲ British cyclist Chris Boardman once cycled more than 35 miles (56 km) in one hour.

▶▶▶ **W**hen people are traveling long distances, they need to know how far they have gone. Cars and motorcycles have a counter on the dashboard that measures the distance traveled. That counter is called an odometer. It works by counting how many times the car's wheels turn around.

Some people have traveled amazing distances to break world records. In 2005, the Trans-USA Challenge driving team drove 5,440 miles (8,755 km) from northern Alaska to southern Florida in 82 hours—a new record. The world record distance traveled on a skateboard is 3,000 miles (4,800 km). It took 26 days to go this far. The longest-ever taxi ride was 21,691 miles (34,706 km).

▲ The distance around the outside edge (marked in yellow) is the wheel's circumference.

Odometers and pedometers

If a car wheel has a circumference of 60 inches (150 cm), each time it turns the car has traveled 60 inches (150 cm). An odometer counts how many times the wheel turns. Since it knows the wheel's size, the odometer can figure out how far the car has traveled. Walkers can place a pedometer on their belt to work out how far they have walked. The device jiggles as they walk, and the pedometer uses the jiggling motion to figure out how far the walker has gone.

FACT

In 2008, Ted McDonald skateboarded 242 miles (387 km) in a day—a world record!

WORD BANK *Circumference: distance round the edge of a circle*

DISTANCES AT SEA

▶▶▶ **F**ar from land—away from landmarks such as lighthouses—it can be difficult for ships to figure out exactly where they are. Navigation involves working out a position at sea or on land. Rough seas and bad weather can make it hard for ships to navigate.

▶ USING SATELLITES

It is much harder to get lost at sea than it was in ancient times. Now there are signals from satellites to help ships navigate. This technology is called GPS, or Global Positioning System. A GPS receiver in a ship picks up signals from four different satellites. In a few seconds, the receiver can figure out a ship's position to within 50 feet (15 meters).

satellite

satellite signal

A ship's GPS receiver picks up signals from four satellites to figure out the ship's exact position.

Sextants and dead reckoning

Since ancient times, people have navigated by looking at the Sun and the stars. A device called a sextant lets people measure how high the Sun is in the sky. From this measurement, a navigator can find out how far north or south the ship is.

If a ship moves at a steady speed in a straight line, sailors can figure out how far the ship has sailed because they know how long it takes to sail one mile at a certain speed. This is called dead reckoning.

▲ This sailor is using a sextant to measure how high the Sun is in the sky. From this measurement, he can figure out exactly where the ship is.

FACT

Modern ships navigate using signals from satellites in space. This method is very accurate.

WORD BANK *Navigation: finding your position at sea or on land*

SPACE DISTANCES

▷▷▷ **S**pace is an enormous place. Most of the things people use to measure distances on Earth cannot be used to measure the immense distances between the stars and planets. Most people find it impossible to imagine what distances in space are really like.

PLANET	DISTANCE FROM SUN
1. Mercury	37 million miles (60 million km)
2. Venus	65 million miles (105 million km)
3. Earth	93 million miles (150 million km
4. Mars	130 million miles (209 million km)
5. Jupiter	484 million miles (778 million km)
6. Saturn	892 million miles (1,436 million km)
7. Uranus	1.78 billion miles (2.87 billion km)
8. Neptune	2.8 billion miles (4.5 billion km)

The illustration is not drawn to scale.

5   6

1   2   3   4

26

Light-years away

One of the closest things to Earth is the Sun, which is 93 million miles (150 million km) away. Some objects in space are much farther away. The closest star to the Sun is 4.3 light-years away. A light-year is the distance that a beam of light travels in a year. It is about 6 trillion miles. It would take a jumbo jet more than one million years to fly that far!

▲ Telescopes can be used to view planets that are millions of miles away from Earth.

FACT

At its closest, the planet Jupiter is 391 million miles (629 million km) from Earth.

▶ SPACE RULERS

When astronauts visited the Moon in the early 1970s, they placed small mirrors on its surface. Scientists on Earth fired laser beams at these mirrors. They used telescopes to time how long the laser beams took to bounce back to Earth. A telescope is an instrument that uses lenses to magnify faraway things. From this result, they measured the distance from Earth to the Moon. It is nearly 250,000 miles (400,000 km).

7   8

9

WORD BANK   *Trillion: one million times one million*

HOW LONG IS YOUR STREET?

YOU WILL NEED

- A piece of ribbon
- Scissors
- A bicycle
- A friend to help you
- An adult to walk with you
- A sharp pencil
- A piece of chalk
- A ruler
- A pen and piece of paper

WHAT TO DO

1. Carefully cut a small length of ribbon using the scissors. Get an adult to help you. Tie the ribbon to the outside of the bicycle tire where you can see it.

2. Turn the bicycle wheel so the ribbon is at the bottom, on the ground. Using the chalk, make a mark on the ground next to the ribbon.

3. Slowly push the bicycle along so the wheel turns around exactly once. The ribbon should move back to the bottom again. With your chalk, make a second mark on the ground, next to the ribbon.

4. Using the ruler, measure the distance between the two chalk marks. This distance is the same as the distance around the edge of your tire, or its circumference. Write down this figure.

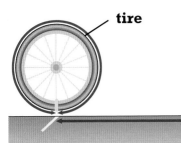
tire

Chalk mark on the street
Ribbon around the tire
Distance between the two chalk marks = circumference of the tire

5. Take your bicycle to one end of your street. Get an adult to go with you. Turn the tire so the ribbon or tape is at the bottom.

6. Wheel the bicycle slowly along from one end of the street to the other. Count how many times the ribbon hits the pavement. That is the number of times the wheel has turned around.

7. Multiply the number of times the wheel turned by the circumference of your tire. For example, say your tire's circumference is 25 inches (62.5 cm) and the wheel has turned around 50 times, the length of your street is:

25 inches x 50
  = 1,250 inches (or 104 feet)

Or: 64 centimeters x 50
  = 3,125 centimeters
  (or 31.25 meters)

GLOSSARY

caliper A device for measuring the distance across (width of) an object.

centimeter A small distance equal to one meter divided by 100.

cubit In ancient times, the distance from the tip of a person's middle finger to their elbow.

distance A measurement of the space between two points. Length measures distance across the ground. Height measures distance from top to bottom.

divider A tool for measuring distances on a map.

foot A distance equal to 12 inches. A foot was originally about the length of an adult's foot.

gauge A device for measuring small widths (distances across things).

inch One-twelfth of a foot. An inch was originally the width of an adult's thumb.

kilometer A metric measurement equal to 1,000 meters.

laser beam A very strong and straight beam of light.

light-year The distance light travels in one year, roughly 6 trillion miles (10 trillion kilometers).

meter A metric measurement equal to about 3.3 feet.

metric A set of measurements based on the meter.

micrometer A very accurate tool for measuring small distances.

microscope A scientific instrument for magnifying very tiny things.

millimeter A very small distance equal to 1 meter divided by 1,000 (or 1 centimeter divided by 10).

mile A distance equal to 5,280 feet, or 1,760 yards (1.6 kilometers).

navigation A way of finding your position on Earth, at sea, or in space.

nanometer An extremely tiny distance; one-billionth of a meter.

ruler A straight measuring tool.

satellite An uncrewed spacecraft that can measure things from space.

sextant A device used for navigating at sea. It measures the position of the Sun above the horizon. The horizon is the farthest part of Earth you can see, where the sky meets the ground.

theodolite A device that people use for measuring distances and angles.

yard A distance equal to 3 feet (90 centimeters).

FIND OUT MORE

BOOKS

Thomas and Heather Adamson, *How Do You Measure Length and Distance?* Mankato, MN: Capstone, 2011.

Brian Cleary, *How Long or How Wide?* Minneapolis, MN: Millbrook, 2007.

Victoria Parker, *How Far Is Far? Comparing Geographical Distances.* Chicago, Il: Heinemann, 2011.

Navin Sullivan, *Area, Distance, and Volume*. New York: Marshall Cavendish Benchmark, 2007.

WEBSITES

Distance conversion chart
Convert volumes from imperial to metric and from metric to imperial.
http://www.sciencemadesimple.com/length_conversion.php

Johnnie's Math Page
Measurement puzzles designed to increase your ability to measure.
http://jmathpage.com/JIMSMeasurementlengthmass volume.html

Publisher's note to educators and parents: Our editors have carefully reviewed these websites to ensure that they are suitable for students. Many websites change frequently, however, and we cannot guarantee that a site's future contents will continue to meet our high standards of quality and educational value. Be advised that students should be closely supervised whenever they access the Internet.

Answers to questions
Page 9: 5 feet 9 inches = 69 inches; 18 feet = 18 x 12 inches = 216 inches; 120 yards = 120 x 3 feet = 360 feet.
Page 13: 4 miles = 6.4 kilometers; 4 inches = 10 centimeters; 16 kilometers = 10 miles.

INDEX

astronaut 27

atoms 17

Boardman, Chris 22

calipers 14, 15

centimeter 11, 12, 13, 19, 21, 23

chains 18, 19, 20

circumference 23

computer 19

cubit 6, 7

dead reckoning 25

dividers 14

Earth 9, 19, 21, 26, 27

Egyptians 6

fingers 6, 7

foot 4, 7, 8, 9, 12, 13, 19, 24

gauges 14, 15

Global Positioning System 24

Greeks 7, 15

height 4, 5

imperial system 9, 10, 11, 13

inch 4, 7, 8, 9, 10, 11, 12, 13, 19, 21, 23

Jupiter 26, 27

kilometer 10, 11, 13, 19, 21, 22, 23, 26, 27

laser beams 5, 19, 27

length 4, 5

lenses 16, 17, 27

light-year 27

maps 4, 14, 20–21

Mars 26

Mercury 26

meter 10, 11, 12, 13, 17, 19, 24

meterstick 12

metric system 10–11, 13

micrometer 15, 17

microscope 16, 17, 18

mile 4, 9, 11, 13, 18, 19, 21, 22, 23, 26, 27

millimeter 11, 13

Moon 4, 27

nanometer 17

nanotechnology 17

nanotubes 17

navigation 24, 25

Neptune 26

odometer 22, 23

pedometer 23

planets 26, 27

pyramid 6

record distances 23

Romans 7, 8

rulers 5, 12–13, 15, 17, 18, 21

satellite 24, 25

Saturn 26

scale 21

sextant 25

ships 24, 25

SI system 10

skateboard 23

sky 25

space 5, 26–27

speed of light 27

stars 25, 26, 27

Sun 25, 26, 27

tapes 5, 12, 18

telescope 27

theodolite 19, 20

thumbs 7, 8

Uranus 26

Venus 26

yard 4, 9, 10, 12, 13

yardstick 12